Mother Goose
A B C

Illustrated by Kinuko Craft

Platt & Munk, Publishers/New York
A Division of Grosset & Dunlap

A diller, a dollar,
A ten o'clock scholar,
What made you come so soon?
You used to come at ten o'clock,
And now you come at noon.

"Baa, baa, black sheep,
Have you any wool?"
"Yes sir, yes sir,
Three bags full:
One for my master,
One for my dame,
And one for the little boy
Who lives down the lane."

Curly Locks, Curly Locks,
Will you be mine?
You shall not wash dishes
Nor feed the swine,
But sit on a cushion
And sew a fine seam,
And feed upon strawberries,
Sugar, and cream.

Daffy-Down-Dilly
Has come to town
In a yellow petticoat
And a green gown.

Elizabeth, Elspeth, Betsy, and Bess,
   They all went together to seek a
      bird's nest;
   They found a bird's nest with five
      eggs in,
   They all took one, and left four in.

Fiddle-de-dee, fiddle-de-dee,
The fly shall marry the bumblebee.
They went to the church,
   and married was she.
The fly has married the bumblebee.

Georgie Porgie, pudding and pie,
Kissed the girls and made them cry;
When the boys came out to play,
Georgie Porgie ran away.

Humpty Dumpty sat on a wall,
Humpty Dumpty had a great fall.
All the king's horses
And all the king's men
Couldn't put Humpty together again.

I saw a ship a-sailing,
    A-sailing on the sea;
And, oh! it was all laden
    With pretty things for thee!

There were comfits in the cabin,
    And apples in the hold;
The sails were made of silk,
    And the masts were made of gold.

The four-and-twenty sailors
    That stood between the decks,
Were four-and-twenty white mice,
    With chains about their necks.

The captain was a duck,
    With a packet on his back;
And when the ship began to move,
    The captain said, "Quack! Quack!"

Jack Sprat could eat no fat,
His wife could eat no lean,
And so, between the two of them,
They licked the platter clean.

King Boggen, he built a fine new hall:
Pastry and piecrust, that was the wall;
The windows were made of black
    pudding and white
Roofed with pancakes—you never saw
    the like.

Little Bo Peep has lost her sheep
And can't tell where to find them.
Leave them alone,
And they'll come home,
Wagging their tails behind them.

Mary, Mary, quite contrary,
How does your garden grow?
With silver bells,
And cockleshells,
And pretty maids all in a row.

North Wind doth blow,
And we shall have snow,
And what will poor Robin do then?
    Poor thing!
He'll sit in the barn,
And keep himself warm,
And hide his head under his wing.
    Poor thing!

Old Mother Goose when
She wanted to wander,
Would ride through the air
On a very fine gander.

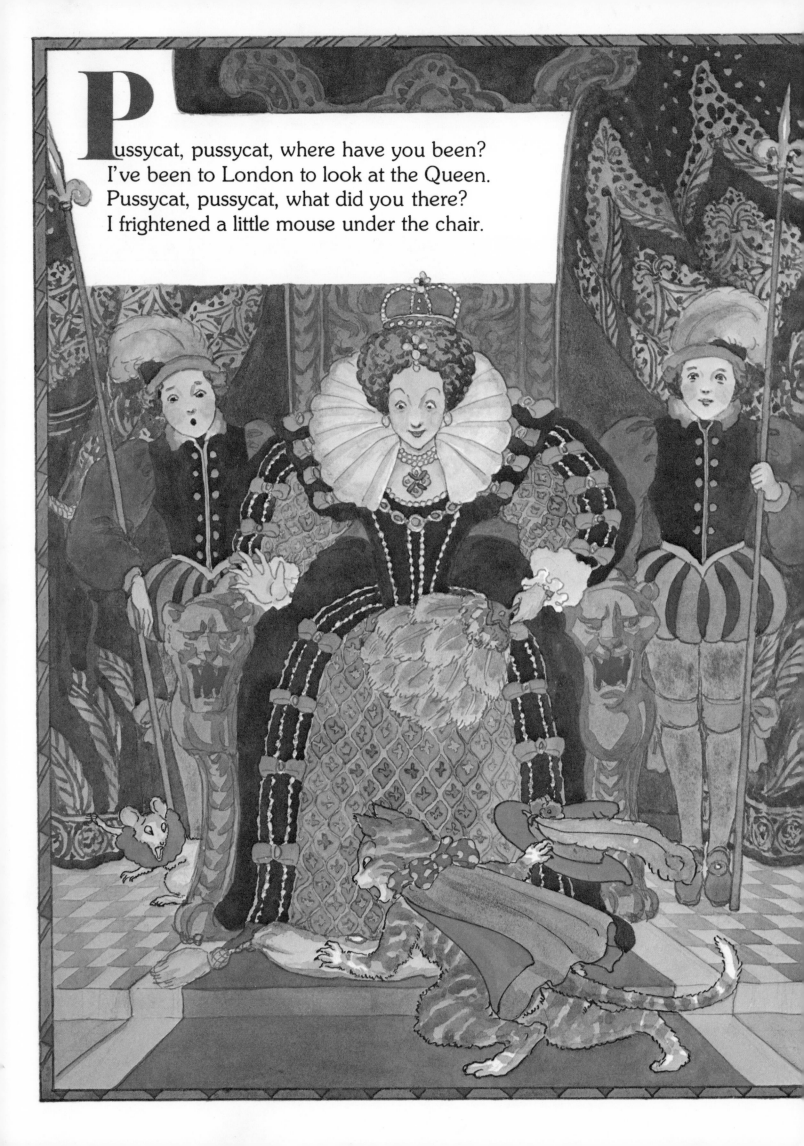

Pussycat, pussycat, where have you been?
I've been to London to look at the Queen.
Pussycat, pussycat, what did you there?
I frightened a little mouse under the chair.

Queen of Hearts
She made some tarts,
  All on a summer's day.
Knave of Hearts
He stole those tarts,
  And took them clean away.

Rub-a-dub-dub,
Three men in a tub,
And who do you think they be?
The butcher, the baker,
The candlestick maker,
They've all gone off on a spree.

Seesaw, Margery Daw,
Johnny shall have
   a new master.
He shall have
   but a penny a day
Because he can't work
   any faster.

There was a crooked man
Who walked a crooked mile,
He found a crooked sixpence
Against a crooked stile.
He bought a crooked cat,
Which caught a crooked mouse,
And they all lived together
In a little crooked house.

U pstairs, downstairs, upon my lady's window,
There I saw a cup of sack and a race of ginger,
Apples at the fire and nuts to crack,
A little boy in the cream pot up to his neck.

V intery, mintery, cutery, corn,
Apple seed and apple thorn;
Wire, brier, limber lock,
Three geese in a flock.
One flew east, one flew west,
And one flew over the goose's nest.

Wee Willie Winkie runs through the town,
Upstairs and downstairs in his nightgown,
Rapping at the window,
Crying through the lock,
"Are the children in their beds,
For now it's eight o'clock?"

X,Y, and tumbledown Z,
The cat's in the cupboard
And can't see me.